I0447742

Time Management

Take Decisive Actions: Achieve your Goals

By Michael Chapman

http://PersonalityDevelopmentMastery.com

PERSONALITY DEVELOPMENT MASTERY

Personality Development Mastery --- ---------- 2016

DISCLAIMER

This book details the author's personal experiences with and opinions about right-brained learning. The author is not licensed as an educational consultant, teacher, psychologist, or psychiatrist.

The author and publisher are providing this book and its contents on an "as is" basis and make no representations or warranties of any kind with respect to this book or its contents. The author and publisher disclaim all such representations and warranties, including for example warranties of merchantability and educational or medical advice for a particular purpose. In addition, the author and publisher do not represent or warrant that the information accessible via this book is accurate, complete or current.

The statements made about products and services have not been evaluated by the U.S. government. Please consult with your own legal or accounting professional regarding the suggestions and recommendations made in this book.

Except as specifically stated in this book, neither the author or publisher, nor any authors, contributors, or other representatives will be liable for damages arising out of or in connection with the use of this book. This is a comprehensive limitation of liability that applies to all damages of any kind, including (without limitation) compensatory; direct, indirect or consequential damages; loss of data, income or profit; loss of or damage to property and claims of third parties.

You understand that this book is not intended as a substitute for consultation with a licensed medical, educational, legal or accounting professional. Before you begin any change in your lifestyle in any way, you will consult a licensed professional to ensure that you are doing what's best for your situation.

This book provides content related to educational, medical, and psychological topics. As such, use of this book implies your acceptance of this disclaimer.

Table of Contents

Introduction

First off, I'd like to thank you for taking the time to download: Time Management: Take Decisive Actions: Achieve your Goals. I know that, given you are reading this book, you are strapped for time or you are not great at managing your own time. If this is the case, then don't worry; you are about to find the easiest, most effective solutions to dealing with this problem once and for all.

How? Because I will show you the most effective time management techniques out there. My name is Michael Chapman, and I can give you all the help that you need with time management. I've learned these skills through my own experience. As someone who manages my own lifestyle and business, I perhaps more than most get to appreciate and see first-hand the massive challenges in time management.

It is by no means an easy feat, or a feat that you can simply click your fingers and become good at. No, becoming more time efficient means taking many years to hone the skills, change your habits and reset your mentality.

This, naturally, takes a lot of time and patience to correctly achieve. If you would like to sort this dilemma out, there comes a time when you have to investigate what's needed. So, together, we'll be looking at;

- **The best tools that you can use to help make your life easier when it comes to time management.**

- **The most effective way to manage your working environment – for most of us, the place we struggle to be at our best is the workplace.**

- **How to get more done, and ensure that success can be consistent.**

- Forming strong plans of action that are bound to make a marginal yet significant difference to your efficiency.

- Various techniques that can come in handy when you wish to operate to the level that you intended.

All of these skills and tricks can easily be used by anyone who wishes to reach that specific level. It means putting in the commitment and the time needed to become more comfortable with who you really are. It also means taking the time to inspect the way that you live, and why you may be the master of your own downfall thus far.

Does this sound like the kind of help that you need? Then let's get started with goal setting!

Goal Setting

The first thing that I want to take a look at is the importance of setting goals. Goal setting is a vital element for anyone who wants to see progressive growth and development in their time management. Without goals, how do you know where to turn to next?

I found that the most effective way for setting goal was going to be quite simple; I just had to understand and appreciate that doing the hardest tasks first always works. Many people mistakenly go for the little jobs first – let me tell you first-hand that this is poor usage of time.

When you take on the little jobs first you can get started and get into a routine, sure. But what about when it comes later on in the day? When the big tasks need to be taken on?

You've already used up energy that you now need for the big jobs later on in the day. You have less time to correct any mistakes or complications that pop up. This makes it nearly impossible to manage your day without fear of failure or slowdowns.

Instead, take the time to start setting some goals. Start with the hardest tasks first, and your days are bound to get easier. Now, when issues go wrong later, it takes minutes to fix the issue rather than hours like before!

To Do Lists

The next solution that you should have on your side is going to be using a to do list, similar to the above. This is something that we will use in the long-term, though. When you set goals for the day like we mentioned above, you should also be looking to set up goals for the weeks ahead. Using a to do list, you can do just that and make your life a whole lot easier in the future.

It just takes a bit of work and planning to get there and make sure you can understand the next step to take on. To do lists usually means putting in the work and the effort to get to where you want to be, and having a path to reach there.

I found that when I started to plan my day using goals from hardest to easiest, my to do lists became easier to write. I could then also build my goals around reaching all of the aims on my list. This was a powerful situation, and one that really make it easy for me to begin working through my tasks one by one.

If you are to make your days and your time more efficient, a to do list will help you begin the process, ensuring that every goal – major or minor – works towards this.

Prioritizing

On your lists and your goals, then, you need to have a priority. As soon as I started noticing that certain tasks would need to be prioritized in a certain order, I began to work harder. Let's use the example of trying to fit piping into a floor. When you go to fit the piping, you wouldn't want to lay all of the new floor and carpet on top first, would you?

Well, you should make sure that every task gets this logic-driven approach to finding a solution to the problem. You should be able to look at the situation you are facing here and come up with a decent solution.

Look at every task you have on your list to get finished by the end of the day. What tasks would need other tasks to be ready before you could take them on? When building your list of goals and things to do, you need to be chronological.

This is why balancing out your tasks based on difficulty can be important. If you get rid of the hardest tasks first by prioritizing the issues that might stop other tasks from being completed, you'll be on the right path.

However, you just have to be prepared for prioritizing tasks to get others completed. As soon as I began doing so, my time management improved tenfold.

Action Plans

Anyone who is serious about taking on all of their goals in a chronological list of priority, then, should see why an action plan may be useful.

You have all of these goals to work through – so how does each get dealt with? Every goal and every task should come with a 10-50-word explanation of how you intend to fix the problem. With so many tasks to do it can become harder to come up with the active and needed solutions all the time. When you are trying to remember how to manage it all, the plan you had to handle certain tasks can escape your mind.

When this happens, it's best to have a little blurb to remind yourself. Even just writing down the person you need to contact or hire for assistance is going to be the easiest way to correcting this issue.

Taking the time to get used to this kind of thinking is very important. Many people don't put much stock in the idea of being so thorough but it really will benefit you in the years to come. One of the most interesting parts of using small explanations on your action plan is that it saves you time making wrong decisions.

When I used to forget, I would guess and waste hours of time trying to create new solutions!

Now, let's take a look at some of the easiest ways you can manage your working environment. Work plays a critical role in all of our lives – so how can you be at your most effective?

Get Rid of Clutter

One of the easiest ways to make your life easier when it comes to work is to get rid of the mess around you. It's ironic that many people see getting rid of mess and clutter as a time waster. They see it as just debris and easily ignored, and taking the hour or so to clean up is a valuable waste of time.

That being said, it's a lot of nonsense!

The most effective thing that you can do for your work space is to keep it clear. This makes it easier to spot the little things you need and keep a more organized desk style. It's important that everything you need is located right next to you – without it, you are merely left to try and find things through a mess!

So, cleaning up is not just being tidy – it's being efficient. Besides, working without all of that mess in your eye-line reduces distractions and this makes you more likely to work. It's a little thing but something as simple as just getting rid of clutter can be all that you need to make your life easier.

Multi-Tasking

The next trick that I can suggest to you is to learn the power of multi-tasking. It's a skill that many people don't feel like they are capable of, and see it as something for other people to mess around with. The problem is that without being able to handle more than one task at the same time, you'll never be efficient.

And no, it's not just for females either! This is a poorly driven myth. You can multi-task so long as you are willing to learn the best way to go about it. This excellent guide from mindtools:
https://www.mindtools.com/pages/article/newHTE_75.htm is well worth checking out, by the way. It will help you see the power of multi-tasking and why you should definitely consider using it in the future.

Personally, I found that learning to handle more than one task at once was a major helping for me. I quickly noticed that I stopped finding it as hard to get multiple tasks per day finished. When I was working on small chunks of each task and chipping away at them all, slowly but surely my work was beginning to get completed as and when I needed it to be.

This is one of the main skills I can recommend to everyone. It's not an impossibility – it's not even extremely challenging. No, the easiest and most effective way to get to grips with multi-tasking is just practice. I would spend one hour per night after work, as soon as I got home, working on my ability to multi-task.

I felt that it was an important step in my development, and I was right. It helped me begin to analyze how I worked, and where I was going wrong. With this plan, then, I began to really take note of how I worked on a daily basis. Before long I was chipping away at the groundwork for all of my major tasks, meaning each working day was more consistent.

Manage Interruptions

I always found that one of the major challenges I had was being able to get rid of and manage interruptions. When I would be working on a task, something would come up. A phone call, my partner, a friend, a colleague – anything at all. Something *always* disrupts our concentration. It's just part of modern life – with so much going on around us, it's hard to expect serenity at all times/

However, to manage interruptions best I found that it was best to put the interruption into the list of priority. Barring obvious emergencies like someone being hurt, an accident or an incident, it can wait. If someone asks you to do something and it's not a priority as of that very second, put it off until you finish what you are doing.

If someone is asking for your help, it's unfair for them to expect you to do it as they demand. They should fall into the next priority, but not your immediate one. The task you were working on before the interruption came along should be the object that receives 100% attention. It's vital that every task that you work on is given your full and utmost concentration.

Without that, you are not giving each of your tasks the right level of mental concentration. However, you can avoid falling into this trap easily enough by keeping your priority on the task at hand. It's a simple mental change and one that I found was incredibly important for me as a person

I used to start worrying about how an interruption would throw the rest of my day. Now, 10% of my mind was worrying about the next problem. Slide in the interruption to your things to do for the day, by all means, but don't let it de-rail where you were before it occurred.

A simple change to make it your next priority, not the current priority, is all you need for efficiency.

Manage Distractions

When an interruption appears it can make it hard to get back to full mental focus, but what about the problems that existed before this came along?

You can't blame interruptions and the need to help others as the sole solution why you are not time efficient. Another major element is distractions – distractions in the form of technology, mainly. When you go to work and are trying to be productive, get the phone off. Turn it off, don't leave it on silent – if you must have it on for emergencies, set a specific phone profile that only vibrates on calls from certain people.

The phone is the main distraction, but I also find that setting the tone is a distraction. Many of us have specific kinds of music we like to work to, but when you get caught up in the music you can spend a lot of time changing the song, for example. I work with a simple audio soundtrack from YouTube, usually music from video games.

Cinematic and instrumental music blends into the cognitive function of our day better than songs. I recommend trying to manage your distractions by limiting the kinds of distractions that you can have. Use music that is functional and not likely to distract you. Change desktop backgrounds on PCs to something bland and dull to avoid it catching the eye. Keep phones on specific sound profiles, face down so you can avoid notifications.

It's the little things that help you manage distractions. My philosophy was simply out of sight, out of mind. Keep yourself open to being alerted of major news and activities, but don't allow distractions to reign around the office.

This can very quickly ruin your chances of being a success in the future. Allowing distractions to stick around is leaving you at the mercy of others, so don't allow yourself to fall into this trap. Instead, manage distractions with an intelligent move towards obscuring them.

Endless Motivation

One of the major challenges I used to face when it came to getting myself into the right frame of mine for helping myself was motivating myself. I used to tell myself that my motivation was to make money, but when I felt financially secure – even temporarily – that motivation would die down. The feeling of achievement used to drive me, too, but once I reached a point of personal success I didn't think I would, I lost that hunger too!

I used to think I had problems with motivation and with the ability to psyche myself up. The problem was that the kind of motivation I was trying to activate was the wrong kind. What you need if you want to have limitless and boundless energy and motivation is an Intrinsic Motivation. What I described above – money, success, grades – are all Extrinsic. Essentially, they are short-term goals that fulfill us temporarily before leaving a pretty big gap for something else to need to come along and fill.

However, to power up that endless motivation, you only need to understand that your sole and total motivation has to come from your inner desires. It's the ability to be free of the burdens of society, and the ability to be our own person. This is what motivates us all – the problem is that we can get too specific when we try to motivate that energy.

We look at how we can empower ourselves with short-term goals, when really our main goal should be happiness. To be more time effective you need to be motivated to complete the task. Well, you need to look at what you have inside you.

I found that my greatest driving factor towards finding my own Intrinsic Motivation came from a desire to make my partner happy. If I was thriving professionally, she'd be happy. When I realized that motivated me more than my ego or desire for success, I never struggled again!

Now that we can see how we can make our work environment more conducive to our success, let's look at how we can get more done per day.

Delegating

One of the most powerful allies that I found in my ability to be more time effective, though, was delegation. I run a company by myself, but I do not work alone. I hire out many of my more menial tasks to people on freelance websites. I go to places like Fiverr, eLance and Freelancer. I hire website designers, I hire content writers, I hire virtual assistants and I hire graphic designers. I have someone who runs my social media campaigns, and I have someone who manages my support e-mails for my services.

This opens up probably the equivalent of a full-time, 40-hours-per-week job worth of time in my working week. I now spend far more time doing what I am best at. All of the skills above? I can do them, with relatively little trouble. However, they all add on hours per day that could be used spending time with my family, working on side-projects, or improving my business.

I don't need to do everything on my own because that's merely charging my ego whilst costing me time. I know that I can do all of this – and having the power to delegate it? That actually gives me more power.

I know that I am doing well enough to get someone else in to help me out. That's a sign of success and of previous efficient time management. So, I now had more time to put 100% into the things I am truly excellent at.

For me, this meant far more than just being involved in the process. It meant that I had time to give my utmost passion and skill to my true passions in life. The other side projects I could do slowly? Now, I let someone with more expertise and output handle it!

Pareto Principle

Another useful skill that I used to turn to with regularity was the Pareto Principle. The Pareto Principle was an ideology named after Vilfredo Pareto, a famous economist. Pareto found that an unequal relationship existed between input, and output. He stated that around 20% of your invested input (in our case, time or money, whatever) is responsible for around 80% of what results that you get.

This is known as the 80/20 rule in many circles, and I found that once learning it, it changed my operational style entirely. There is no balance between what you put in and what you get out of a subject most of the time. This can be something that leaves a lot of people uncertain about the time they should put into something – myself included.

80% of your entire output might come from just 20% of the work that you put in. That might seem frustrating but it's better to acknowledge it. Now, you can see that time management is very important – making that 20% the best 20% it can be is going to be so incredibly important. So, to become more time efficient, the 20% responsible for your 80% output should get as much of your commitment mentally as it can.

That isn't to say that you slack off on the other 80%, but your time should be magnified on that 20% especially. Whilst you still need a good and fair balance across the board, prioritization is a vital nature to maintain sustained, continued success.

This is very important to note as many people try and give 100% to everything, then wonder why results don't improve. Every business and every person has an imbalanced avenue towards success. The sooner you can see this and balance that out, the sooner you can begin to correct these issues.

As soon as I became aware of this and changed tact accordingly, my business has continually seen marginal improvements across the 20%.

So, now that we can appreciate the unique and challenging landscape of getting more done, let's take a look at creating a plan of action.

Small Tasks

The first part of your plan of action, as we have already looked at, should come from managing small tasks. You should always look to make smaller tasks a later part of your plan in any given day. When something goes wrong with a smaller task it can take you minutes to find the solution. When it goes wrong with a larger task, though, the solution can be that little bit harder to come across.

Whatever the scenario you find unfolding, though, managing small tasks is a very important barometer of where you are going to be heading in the future. Any good plan of action should take into account the importance of larger tasks first and foremost. They are usually the tasks that require the hardest work and have the largest chance of failing – for that reason, making them the priority should be something you start gradually doing.

That being said, sometimes a small task has to be completed to open up the path to taking on a larger task. If that's the case then it's not a problem – so long as you can complete everything needed to finish that larger task, it's worth the deviation in time and effort. Just remember that small tasks should always be the second priority after the larger tasks, unless it's a precursor.

The reason why this helps so much is that when we make a mistake on a large task, we'll struggle. Finding a solution could take you hours – when this goes wrong at the end of the day, it ruins the next day for you as well. If you need to catch up on a few smaller tasks the day after a problem the so be it but it should never be managing your main tasks a day later than expected.

Always make the priority count if you want to see continued gains from managing small tasks. It's a challenge and one that will likely push you beyond your typical limits, but once you get used to it then it will become a lot less of an issue in future.

Organization and Procrastination

Many people believe that by putting something off, they are organizing it. I used to do it myself. "I'm not at 100% on this, would rather come back at it from a new angle tomorrow" but the more you do this, the worse it gets. I would always find myself losing track of time and, before long, my procrastination would lead to exceptional rush-jobs and loss of quality in the things that I do.

Naturally, this is not what you want to happen when working on a project. So, I decided to make some comprehensive changes to the way that I worked and the way that I would plan. To do this, I looked into the major difference between organization, and procrastination.

- **When you organize something, you are preparing in the short-term the tools needed to do the best job that you can.**

- **When you procrastinate, you are putting the organization off until another day. When you procrastinate you are making excuses, not organizing**

This is a major distinction and one that you have to go pretty far to find a reason for. It takes a long time and will usually mean that you have to look at how you handle these kinds of situations more readily in the future. With that in mind, then, you need to take a look at what happens when you put off beginning a task.

Do you actually get to work on the planning aspect?

Or do you just ignore it until tomorrow?

For those who do the former, you are organizing – the latter is procrastination. If you don't begin work on the day that you intended on a project, that's fine. Just make sure that you spend that day preparing the groundwork for the day that you do begin. Any day spend doing nothing to enhance a project is a day wasted – remember that.

My main recommendation would always be to make sure that your plan of action leaves clear gaps for organizational days. When you just plan to start on day X, you can procrastinate. Make time for organization, and you'll procrastinate less.

The Reasons Behind Procrastination

So, still not sure if you are procrastinating or coming up with the next superstar plan? This should help you see the easiest way to fix that distinction in your mind. I'm going to show you the main reasons why someone may procrastinate and what drives us to act and think like this in the future.

It Becomes a Habit

The most common reason is because we allow it to exist in our mindset. Many people simply procrastinate because that is all that they know – they spend all of their time in this hazy bubble. When you are used to being five minutes late, paying bills on the wrong day and missing opportunities you just let it become part of you.

Failing to Estimate

Many of us procrastinate, though, because we cannot evaluate time accordingly. To become better at managing your time you have to estimate your time better. Be more pessimistic in your timing. Rather than always estimating that you will complete a task in your best time, estimate that you will complete it in your worst time. Then, you continually surprise yourself and gain motivation instead of letting yourself down, and losing it.

Addictive Personalities

Those who procrastinate seem to take everything in larger doses than they once intended. From getting involved with an addictive substance to simply having a few glasses of juice more than intended, procrastination is part of being an addictive personality. You usually find yourself supplementing your mindset with a lack of self-regulation, and this drips into your time.

Easily Distracted

The other main reason is that people can become very easily distracted and this creates procrastination. As we spoke about earlier, access to friends and family, social media, news sites and eCommerce makes it easy to find ourselves distracted today.

So, I found the best solution for me was a very simple one. I accepted that each of the attributes above played a part in my lifestyle. Once I recognized the mini problems contributing to a major personality flaw, I knew that I had something to start working on – do you?

Managing your Inbox

A big issue for me was a major inability to manage my email inbox. I would find myself wasting an hour or two per day sifting through e-mails looking for the ones that matter. So, I decided to take the initiative. Instead of losing one hour per day looking through e-mails, I lost three or four hours in one day changing my entire e-mail setup.

I downloaded e-mail plugins for Gmail that helped to avoid spam. I spent time making tags and filters for colleagues, friends, family and work. I made sure that spam was sent to the right place. I created custom notifications for my e-mails to make sure that the higher the priority, the more likely it was that I would spot the notification faster.

The quicker the important emails were spotted, the faster I could build a legitimate response to the person waiting for me. This was so important and was a major driver in my business becoming stronger, and my time becoming more efficient.

By simply taking the time to make my e-mail inbox more lively and easier to work with, I found that it rapidly changed the structure of how I was working. Not only did this make a significant contribution to the way that I was working, but it helped me to become more secure in who I was missing out on.

I used to always fear that I'd missed important e-mails due to the influx of spam. So, I would spend lots of time just searching for potential e-mails I was expecting but never received. This meant that I wasted lots of time chasing phantom e-mails.

Thankfully, this was all changed relatively quickly when I adjusted how I let my inbox control itself. This changed how I was likely to manage my inbox and where I was likely to go in the future with this kind of thinking.

It might seem small, but it's another useful cog in a time effective action plan.

Stop Wasting Time in Meetings

A common issue that I tended to have as well in my lack of time efficiency was handling meetings. I'm a fairly informal and social guy, so I found it quite easy to turn a 30-minute meeting into an hour and 30 minutes.

We would do this just by chatting away and getting sidetracked. For me, it was networking and solidifying the relationship that I had with my clients – and believe me, it worked!

The only problem was that whilst it worked, I was spending way too much time per day doing nothing.

My meetings were overlapping and becoming a bit of a major issue. I was going from one chat to the next, never filing in my mind what my clients were telling me. It became a bit of a struggle and I was making semi-common mistakes and forgetting parts of the meeting.

That might brutally unprofessional, but it was just a side-product of not looking after time enough. Being too time-friendly with clients was making me lose track of meetings and progress. I was coming out remembering the laughs we had more than the programs we agreed upon!

Now, this became a major issue for me. I fixed it simply by setting a limit of 10% overspill for any meeting. So, a 30-minute meeting could last at most 33-minutes. This allowed for me to spend a bit of time gabbing with clients, but still having plenty of time to get to the next meeting all in good time.

Naturally, this kind of thing becomes increasingly important as time goes on and I found that most of my clients appreciated that side to me – I was giving, but not just there to talk about the kids and soccer. It made a big difference to my overall time output, and made sure that my action plans each day slowly but surely began to mature to fit with the model I wanted to run.

Apply the 80/20 Rule

Earlier on, we mentioned the 80/x02 rule. As part of your plan of action, you should be using the 80/20 rule as a bit of a guiding light. Not only is this kind of ruling very useful for becoming more time efficient but it's bound to make sure that you continue to see more progress as a person.

To start with, I want you to go and get a piece of paper or open up a blank document. Now, crack those fingers and write down the ten things in your life you wish to achieve long-term. These are things that you see as vital cogs to your happiness, security and personal wealth. However, once they are written down, you need to ask yourself something.

Find out, in your mind, what the goal you wish to accomplish most would be. If you had to pick just one of those goals to accomplish today – what would it be? And why?

Write that down next, too. The goal that you pick should be the one that will have the most telling, and lasting, positive effect on your life. Any other choice is simply rolling the dice and hoping for the best. The 80/20 rule is all about finding the one thing that makes the biggest difference. This is the opposite of marginal gains, where you use lots of little 1% improvements to make a big change.

No, with the 80/20 rule you are looking to find one thing that you can change that improves many other elements of your life. Once you have finished picking that task, pick the second most important task – these are now the 20% that you need to accomplish.

So long as both goals are going to help you accomplish the other 80%, you have applied the rule!

Learn to say NO

If you are anything like me, then you no doubt waste a lot of time being unable to say no. I used to lose hours both in my old job and in running my own business taking on odd jobs I didn't have to. Why? Because someone asked.

Through fear of offending a friend or annoying a client, I would take on crazy tasks. From helping to build a small brick wall (terribly) to writing e-mail scripts for a client, I spend a lot of my time doing tasks I shouldn't be. This is a big problem for me and it was one of the first things I changed about myself when I was made aware of the damaging effect it was having on my life.

As soon as I learned to say no, it was likely a revolution. I started finishing tasks on time, and I found that my biggest fear – letting others down – evaporated. Nobody seemed to be angry at me for not jumping to dance to their tune, as I expected. In fact, it would appear that the extra work I was completing due to having more time to myself was making a bigger impact on their lives instead.

The only thing I can say here to help you get by always saying no is that people won't turn on you. And if someone does, they aren't worth fretting over. It's better to lose a poor friend than keep one, and it's the same with a client. If your time management is out of sync because you keep going above and beyond with no real reward, stop doing it.

Anyone who turns on you for not doing as they demand is not worth worrying about anyway! Change your mentality, say no, and you'll be far more time-efficient. This change in mentality can really go a long way to helping you reach the level you want to, whilst removing a negative character trait.

Alright, so now we've looked at how to form a good plan of attack, let's look at how to make that plan stronger with supplementary techniques and ideas.

Attacking the Day

The best way to make sure that you get the most out of your time is to be up bright and early. I found that the easiest way to do this was to create a sleeping pattern that gave me my maximum hours needed.

Since I don't have a hugely physically demanding job (apart from when I used to build walls out of kindness!) I usually get by on 6-7 hours of sleep. I also like the peace and quiet of night, so do a lot of my recreational activities towards the little hours of the morning. This meant that I had to adjust my days to be ready to be attacked.

It's all well and good saying I'll be in the office and working for 9AM, but if I only go sleep at 2:30AM it's not going to be a good fit – not for long. Instead, I compromised and made the fair balance of creating a guarantee of starting work every morning at 11AM. This gave me enough time to have the lifestyle I wanted and made sure that I started the day ready to roar into life.

Although it's a small distinction but one that made a huge difference for me. To attack the day, you need to be up and ready to start at an hour that fits your lifestyle. If you need to be up earlier, then you have to go to bed earlier and get enough rest. You'll be attacking nothing if you don't have the energy to do so, that's for sure!

This makes a massive difference to your overall chances of success. When you get up at a good time and go to work accordingly ready to attack the day, you'll be more efficient with your time and your task completion rates.

Optimizing Working Pace

One of the major challenges for most people is also finding out how to organize a fair and optimal working pace. We all like to believe we can always work at our operational peak, but there's no guarantee. This is what we spoke of in procrastination – when you expect to always work at 100% efficiency, you think you can cut more time into breaks and sitting around enjoying relaxation.

It's not the case, though, because none of us work at our very best working pace. Therefore, it helps to try and create a consistent balance with a happy, optimal working pace. This, though, can be quite challenging to work out and appreciate because everyone has different jobs, lifestyles, ambitions and needs.

I recommend that if you want to make an optimal working speed, you look at your fastest working pace and knock 20% off of it. That allows for days when things are slow, when you aren't at it, or when you have other problems to contend with. This makes a big difference and can help out quite a long way in making sure that you start creating an appetite for consistency.

Now you feel under less pressure to always work at an unsustainable medium. You start to hit targets more often, you stay on time more regularly, and feel better about yourself. Never compare yourself to the best days that you have as it's unfavorable. Working conditions and life conditions change, and reaching those very best days is tough work.

Don't expect to always just hit the right levels that you can at your very best. It's not as simple as that – you should always judge yourself just below your optimum. This allows for greater time efficiency but removes the challenging emotional burden of not hitting the levels that you unrealistically demand of yourself.

Therefore, it can be quite a liberating feeling to find a pace that isn't pushing you beyond your actual limits.

Keep your Day Planned

The best solution that I can offer for those who want to see greater solutions and time-efficiency improvements is to plan out your day accordingly. We've mentioned the importance of having quality action plans and dealing with the smaller tasks first, but how else can you go about planning your day?

- Start off by planning the things you need to deal with – food, hygiene and work. Keep these as the top priorities and make sure that you build in the right level of performance. Don't leave half an hour for lunch if your lunch takes 25 minutes to cook, for example. Make sure that you are fair with time and that you are happy to see time elsewhere being eaten into to make up for that.

- Set together a fair plan for things to do recreationally. We are more likely to stay motivated when we know we have, say, a games night with friends waiting for us at the end of the day than another night of randomness. It helps to make a bit of a regiment for the week, as it ensures that even recreational activity can be used as part of the day – something to look forward to at the end of it, mainly.

- Another great way to make sure you stick to the plan of the day is to leave gaps for errors. Try and create a time frame of around 1 hour/1 hour and a half to allow for mistakes and problems. This can be anything from food taking longer to cook to the internet being off and slowing down your working day.

- Make sure that every day you plan out runs in an order which isn't unrealistic. Don't expect yourself to be able to keep pace with another member of your team who is more experienced, for example. Always build your day's plan around what you are capable of achieving; so long as you reach those standards, you'll be happy.

Drink Water

I used to spend most of my time drinking soda during the day. I wanted a little sugary treat to keep me going. All this led to was damaged teeth, short energy levels and a craving for sugar during the day that limited my productivity. When a friend recommended I switch to good old water, I was quite suspicious.

However, the difference it makes is pretty crazy. When our body has enough water to function and run with then we can concentrate and plan tasks accordingly. When you have a set of instructions to follow it becomes a whole lot easier to get to grips with what the instructions say. We can take in, understand, retain and then act on information far more with a good water intake than we can without.

I recommend buying some re-fillable water bottles online that you can take to and from the office with you. This makes it much easier to take regular sips and keep your water levels high throughout the day. The difference it makes is really quite impressive. I found that I was able to give my brain the help it needed to retain information by doing this.

Since I am also free of dehydration at this point, my body operates much smoother than it would have without it. Not only is this going to massively and rapidly improve overall performance but it's going to make me feel a lot healthier as well.

If you find that your days get bogged down in confusion as soon as new information comes along, try drinking more water. Setbacks should be something that you can deal with and having a hydrated and well looked after body can do that for you.

This is going to really help make your days in general fly in. You'll be more productive and also much more likely to positively react to a setback. If you're days seem a struggle, try drinking more water.

Make Checklist

I've been quite clear throughout this that using a checklist is very important. Having access to this kind of solution for each day – prepared before bed the night before –is invaluable. Not only is it going to make it much easier for you to arrange a solution with yourself as much as anything else, but it's going to make sure that your day has a key structure.

Make sure that every day carries ten tasks minimum that you need to get through. In any given time period you should be able to clear them all. Make sure that the tasks are selected in accordance with the time that you have, and if you can afford to delegate any then you should. Making a checklist means that at the end of the day you will never miss out on something important.

It's so easy to accidentally forget to handle a minor task that would become a major problem come the next day. So, you can easily deal with this problem simply by making a small checklist to follow along with and agree to. It's going to ensure that you get much closer to being more efficient with your time.

To make the best checklists, I do heavily recommend that you use a mobile app. You can get lots of great mobile checklist apps, or even just a notepad on your device. This lets you record the challenges of each day ahead and also how you got through each task.

This is important as it helps to build a clear record of what you achieve each and every day, and what you had to leave for next time.

I would also fully recommend that you make a checklist on the basis that it minimizes the amount of work you need to put into managing your long-term goals. It's easier to reach what you see as your final destination when each day is ticking off various important tasks!

Replacing your Mindset

I always found that one of my major problems, at least at the start of my professional career, was an inability to get revved up for activities. If something came along that could potentially make me a better professional, assist me in networking or teach me something new I would avoid it.

Why?

Because I had convinced myself that I had such a hard day and that I needed some rest. Always telling myself that "I am busy" was much easier to contend with in the head than putting myself out there.

My plan was simple, yet pathetic in equal measure. I would look to find excuses to avoid extracurricular activity as I was scared it would take as much time as my poorly managed working day would. I have no shame or fear in admitting that this was a problem for me, and one that really held me back.

To make sure that this problem could be avoided in the future, then I began to work to slowly replace that mindset. If you are like me and don't know where to start, then make the change in an aspect of life that isn't professional, for example. Do you tend to avoid nights out or social events? Then put yourself out there for a few days.

It will help you see that things can be fun when you expected they wouldn't be. Your expectations can be wrong, and simply challenging your go-to response to something outside of your comfort zone is a good way to prove that!

My main recommendation for replacing a "too busy" with a "let's do it!" mentality is to simply take more risks. Something might not work out for you, and it could be a waste of valuable time, and money. But what if it's not?

I simply had to change how I viewed the next step forward in my life. When I took the excruciating steps needed to improve this, I found taking risks soon became fun!

Taking Things One At A Time

Are you someone who tries to give 5% to 20 different things? If so, it's no wonder you are poor with your time!

The best way to correct this issue is to simply start looking at taking things one thing at a time. You see in professional sports that coaches are very strict on a one game at a time mantra. Why? Because when we start looking too far ahead, we lose track of the little details.

You could be so obsessed with the long-term end game that you lose sight of the 'easy' task in front of you. How often does a sports team who are in a good run of form fall over at a supposedly simple challenge? They do this because their minds weren't 100% concentrated on the job in hand.

If you want to become the best that you can be, you have to start working on everything at 100%. Taking an hour to do 20 tasks at 1 hour each is better than making tiny minute adjustments to them all at once.

It simply doesn't get you anywhere and is likely to see your progress outreached by others who give 100% to that one task.

Making small progress in lots of tasks is not a viable solution if you want to be efficient with your time. It's different If tIme Is of no issue to you, but when the clock is ticking taking everything on their own merits is vital.

I found that my strongest solution to this was to simply remove all inference to the task after the one I was operating on. It soon became a whole lot easier to look after my performance and to make sure that I was getting closer to finishing tasks properly.

When you offer just a few moments to a task it's unlikely to get finished at 100% quality. Give it your all today, though, and it will be finished the best it possibly can be.

Picture Your Return

A very easy way to lose track of time and your overall efficiency is to get caught up in your holidays. When we jet off for time off we usually just put all of our work thoughts to the side when we return. As amicable as this may be to go and recharge your batteries, it's not really the best solution of all time!

Making a clear and obvious picture in your head of what awaits you when you return is very important. Your current work that you are operating on will still be waiting for you by the time that you get back. This is going to go very far to making sure that you can correct the issues that await when you get return, too – simply forgetting about it solves nothing.

Instead, I would recommend that you spend some time getting used to the idea of picturing what waits you on your return. Taking a clear note of the things you still need to do for your first day back, on the day that you finish, is so helpful.

When you return after a time of not thinking about work you'll have likely forgotten where you had gotten to at that point. So, how do you deal with this?

I simply made a note and a list of everything I could have potentially changed before I left for holiday. This means that when I get back I have a small listing of things to work on, and ideas to implement. This was very important, helping me to drive towards creating a successful and happy range of solutions to take on when I got home.

It was a simple change and one I felt was very useful. If you are like me and find yourself falling behind for the first few days – or even the first week – back, then try this out. Having a little list pre-prepared when you are still in full work mode is better than trying to remember after a weekend by the beach!

www.ingramcontent.com/pod-product-compliance
Lightning Source LLC
Chambersburg PA
CBHW070244290526
45789CB00004B/1750